TECHNOLOGY THEN AND NOW

COMPUTERS
THEN AND NOW

CYNTHIA KENNEDY HENZEL

childsworld.com

The Child's World
childsworld.com

Published by The Child's World®
800-599-READ • www.childsworld.com

Photography Credits
Photographs ©: Shutterstock Images, cover (background), cover (left computer), cover (icon), 1 (background), 1 (left computer), 1 (icon), 3 (background), 3 (icon), 4, 11, 13, 14; Den Rozhnovsky/Shutterstock Images, cover (right computer), 1 (right computer); DC Studio/Shutterstock Images, cover (game), 1 (game); Everett Collection/Shutterstock Images, 5; Trong Nguyen/Shutterstock Images, 7; Monkey Business Images/Shutterstock Images, 8, 16–17; Hananeko Studio/Shutterstock Images, 18; Red Line Editorial, 20

ISBN Information
9781503889514 (Reinforced Library Binding)
9781503891135 (Portable Document Format)
9781503892378 (Online Multi-user eBook)
9781503893610 (Electronic Publication)

LCCN 2023950442

Printed in the United States of America

BRINGING THE WORLD TO YOUNG READERS 1968

Cynthia Kennedy Henzel has a BS in social studies education and an MS in geography. She has worked as a teacher-educator in many countries. Currently, she writes fiction and nonfiction books and develops educational materials for social studies, history, science, and ELL students. She has written more than 100 books and 150 stories for young people.

TABLE OF CONTENTS

THE HISTORY OF COMPUTERS

In the 1940s, the British built the first **electronic** computers. They used them to break German codes during World War II (1939–1945). In the United States, the military built the Electronic Numerical Integrator and Computer (ENIAC). It could do 5,000 additions per second. It needed 1,800 square feet (167 sq m) of space. Today's computers can be smaller than a grain of rice. They can do a huge number of **calculations** per second. They provide entertainment and information. People use them to communicate. Computers keep companies and governments running.

Computer technology is always changing. Soon, people will use computers in new and more powerful ways.

CHAPTER 1

PERSONAL COMPUTERS

In the 1960s, Jack Kilby invented the **microchip**. This allowed computers to get smaller and cheaper. Now, companies could make personal computers (PCs) to sell. Most early PCs had no **graphics**. Users had to type instructions to open a **program**.

Steve Jobs and Steve Wozniak started a company called Apple in 1976. They thought computers should be easier to use. In 1977, Apple created the Apple II computer. The Apple II had new color graphics and a built-in speaker for sound.

The basic version of the Apple II sold in 1977 for $1,298, equal to $6,397 in 2023.

Computers gave teachers new ways to help students learn.

Apple said that this PC could help people manage their money. By 1984, more than 2 million Apple II computers had sold.

Kids loved the games that came with the Apple II. In *Lemonade Stand*, players ran a lemonade stand for money. People wondered whether computers could help kids learn. The Minnesota Educational Computing Consortium (MECC) believed that computers had a place in learning. It worked with Apple to put computers in Minnesota schools. It also trained teachers and provided **software**. The MECC was so successful that it began to make and sell video games. It also worked to put computers in classrooms across the country.

In 1985, Microsoft created the Windows **operating system** to make using computers easier. Windows 3 was released in 1990 and sold millions of copies. It was used on lots of computers. These included computers made by the company IBM.

CHAPTER 2

THE INTERNET

The internet is a system that connects computers together. The military and some universities had connected computers in the 1960s. But the internet became public in 1992. That year, Tim Berners-Lee released the World Wide Web. The "web" is a way for internet users to communicate. On the web, each web page has a unique address. It is called a URL.

The web allowed anyone with a computer to put information on the internet. But finding that information was difficult. More than 2 million websites existed by 1998.

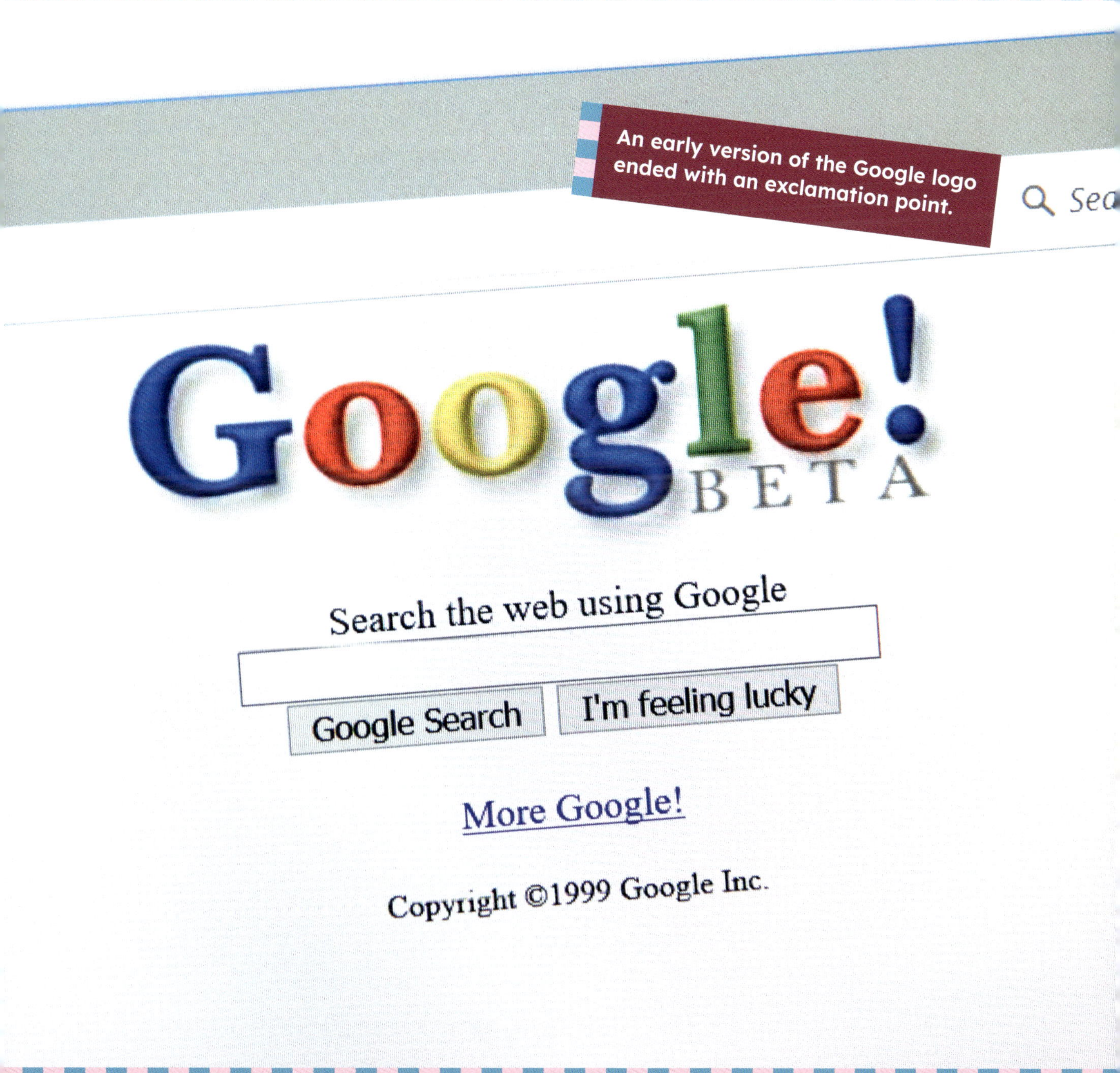

An early version of the Google logo ended with an exclamation point.

To help people find information on the web, Larry Page and Sergey Brin created Google. Users could type **keywords** into the Google site. Google software located websites that matched the keywords. Google also put websites in order for the user.

More and more people went **online**. Amazon and eBay opened for business in 1995. They were the biggest online marketplaces. The company PayPal opened in 1998. It provided a safe way to send money online.

The internet changed the way people found information. The Encyclopedia Britannica went online in 1994. CNN, a news network, went online the next year.

The website Wikipedia was created in 2001.

The internet also changed entertainment. People could buy music on the internet. The video game *World of Warcraft* was released in 2004. Soon, it had millions of players. Netflix began streaming movies to people's TVs in 2007.

THE RISE OF EMAIL

In the 1990s and 2000s, email changed the way people communicated. Things that used to be sent as real mail could now be sent over the internet. Messages sent over email arrive almost instantly.

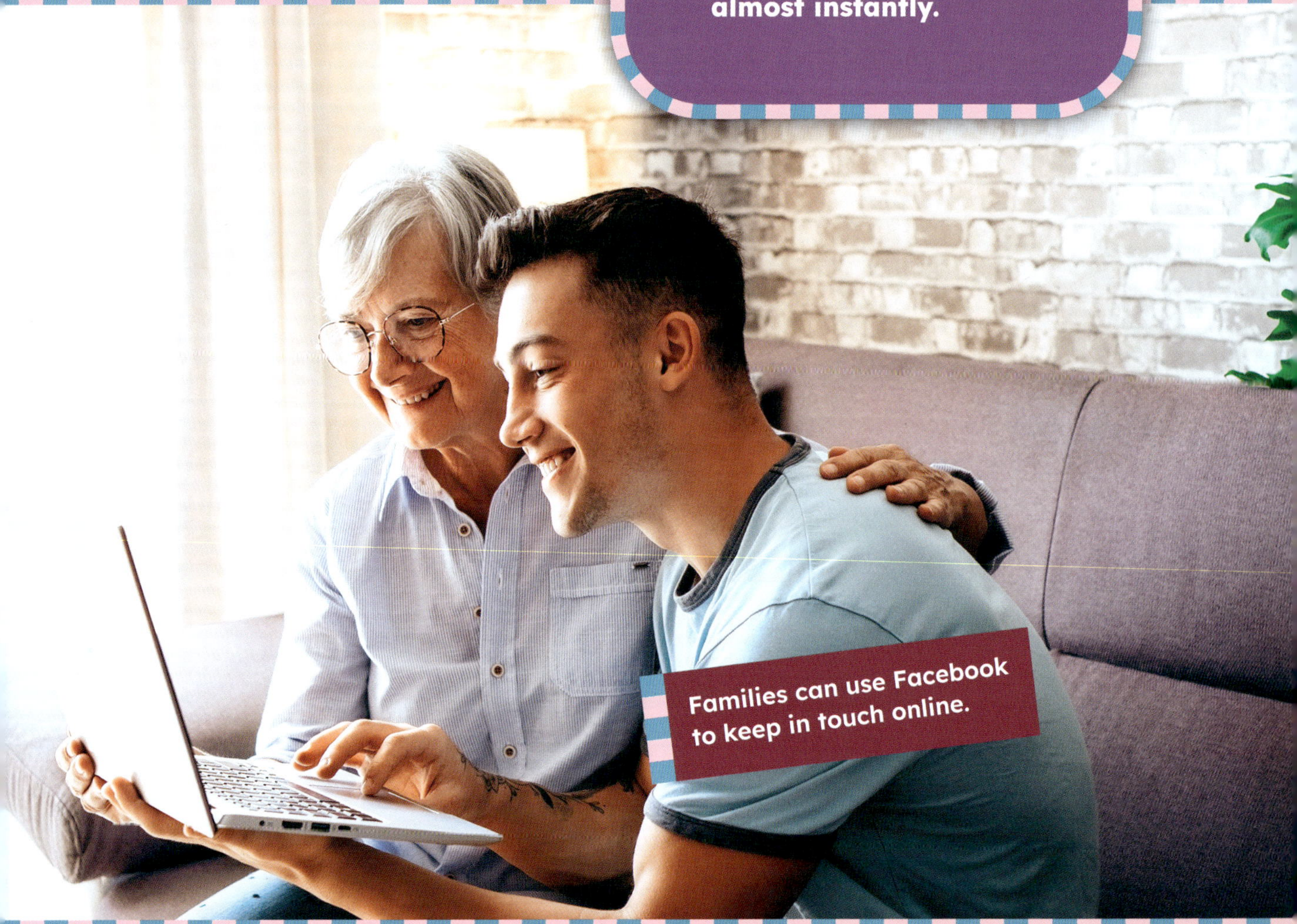

Families can use Facebook to keep in touch online.

People could communicate on the internet, too. They could send emails. Social media websites allowed people to talk and share content. Myspace launched in 2003. It was one of the first big social media networks. Facebook followed in 2004. By 2005, 69 percent of adults and 90 percent of teenagers in the United States had used the internet.

CHAPTER 3

EVERYTHING IS ONLINE

Today, society depends on computers. People use computers to run banks, hospitals, and schools. People shop and pay bills online. They keep in touch with friends. Facebook had 3 billion users in 2023. It was the largest social media site that year. People use programs such as Zoom for meetings and doctor appointments. In 2023, about 92 percent of Americans used the internet.

Computers are a common sight in workplaces today.

Many students in elementary school took classes online due to COVID-19.

In 2020, COVID-19 shut down many schools and businesses. Students went to school online. Many adults started working online from home. Eventually, most students went back to in-person class. But computers have not gone away. Teachers make and collect assignments online. They provide reading materials. They communicate with students and their parents.

Computers have created problems. People can put false information online. This might affect how people think and vote in elections. Some people use computers to steal private information. Attacks on computer systems can seriously harm companies or governments.

INTERNET USAGE OVER TIME

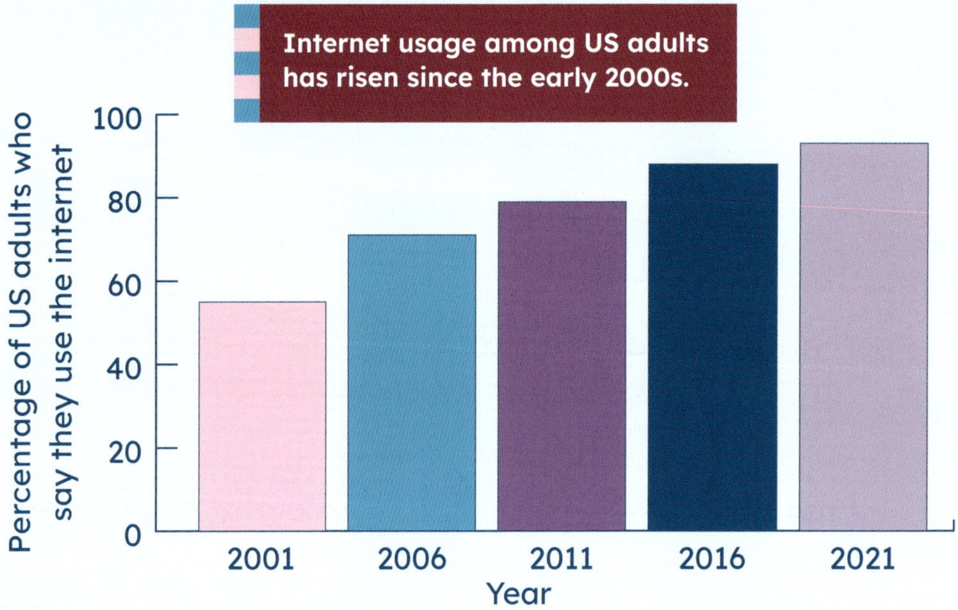

Artificial intelligence (AI) is a new computer technology. It is changing the way people live and work. AI is the ability of computers to learn. It works by giving computers large amounts of information. AI allows computers to do tasks that people commonly do. These tasks could include driving a car or writing a news report. In the future, society may depend on AI to do many jobs that people do today.

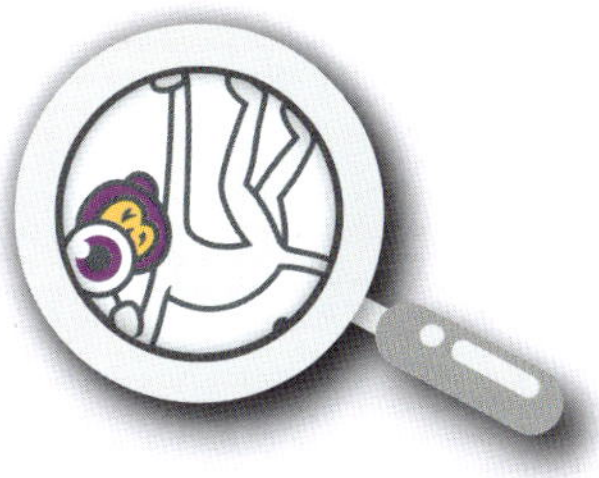

WONDER MORE

Wondering about New Information

How much did you know about the history of computers before reading this book? What new information did you learn? Write down three new facts that this book taught you. Was the new information surprising? Why or why not?

Wondering How It Matters

What is one way computers relate to your life? If you cannot think of a personal connection, imagine a way computers might affect other kids. What impact might they have on their lives?

Wondering Why

Computer systems are very complex. Why do you think it is important for people who use these systems to follow rules? Do you think computer companies, governments, or someone else should make rules for using computers? Why?

Ways to Keep Wondering

Computers can be used for good or bad reasons. After reading this book, what questions do you have about relying on computers? What can you do to learn more about how computers affect daily life?

FAST FACTS

- The first computers were used by the military.
- After the invention of the microchip, computers got small enough to use in homes.
- Computers got easier to use and gained more graphics and programs over time.
- The Apple II was the first computer widely used in schools.
- Microsoft released Windows in 1985. Later versions of Windows sold very well.
- Google was released in 1998. It gave people easy access to information.
- By the early 2000s, there were businesses for online shopping, gaming, and social networking.
- By the 2020s, computers were everywhere. They were used to run major systems such as utilities, banks, and companies.
- People can misuse computers by stealing personal information and promoting false information.
- New AI technology is changing the way people use computers.

GLOSSARY

calculations (kal-kyuh-LAY-shunz) Calculations are answers to math problems. Computers can do calculations very quickly.

electronic (ee-lek-TRAH-nik) A device is electronic if it works using electricity. Computers are electronic.

graphics (GRA-fiks) Graphics are pictures made on computers. Most modern video games have graphics.

keywords (KEE-wurds) Keywords are words typed into a search program to find a website. Google uses keywords to sort search results.

microchip (MY-kroh-chip) A microchip is a tiny computer part that processes information. A new microchip can be small but very powerful.

online (awn-LYNE) Online means using the internet to do something. People can play video games with others online.

operating system (AH-puh-ray-ting SIS-tum) An operating system is a program that manages a computer's basic functions. Windows is a widely used operating system.

program (PRO-gram) A program is a set of instructions for a computer. Lots of computers come with a calculator program.

software (SAWFT-wayr) Software is the set of programs that a computer uses. Video games are a kind of software.

FIND OUT MORE

In the Library

Bethea, Nikole Brooks. *How Does the Internet Work?* Minneapolis, MN: Jump!, 2020.

Humphrey, Natalie. *Making a Computer.* Buffalo, NY: Rosen, 2024.

Williams, Dinah. *Artificial Intelligence.* New York, NY: Starry Forest Books, 2021.

On the Web

Visit our website for links about computers:
childsworld.com/links

Note to Parents, Caregivers, Teachers, and Librarians: We routinely verify our web links to make sure they are safe and active sites. So encourage your readers to check them out!

INDEX